Distant Lands: An Anthology of Poets Who Don't Exist

DISTANT LANDS
An Anthology of Poets Who Don't Exist

Agnieszka Kuciak

Translated by Karen Kovacik

WHITE PINE PRESS / BUFFALO, NEW YORK

White Pine Press
P.O. Box 236
Buffalo, New York 14201
www.whitepine.org

Acknowledgments:
Earlier versions of "Arrival at Byzantium," "In Rome," "Naked, she let me in a secret gate," "Parable," "Romance," and "Waiting for the Blondes." appeared in the anthology *Six Polish Poets*, edited by Jacek Dehnel (Todmorden, U.K.: Arc Publications, 2008).

Two other earlier versions, "Depression" and "The rain knocks long on everything," were co-translated with Ewa Chrusciel; I'm very grateful for our conversations about those poems.

Publication of this book has been subsidized by Instytut Książki - the ©POLAND Translation Programme, and was made possible, in part, by grants from the National Endowment for the Arts, which believes that a great nation deserves great art; with public funds from the New York State Council on the Arts, a State Agency.

Cover art and design: Olgierd Chmielewski

First Edition.

ISBN: 978-1-935210-45-0

Printed and bound in the United States of America.

Library of Congress Control Number: 2012948060

Contents

III. In the House of the Psyche

IV. Resurrection Rhymes and Other Poems

Preface

The complaint about Henry James—okay, one of the many complaints—is that when his characters speak, they all sound alike, that is, they all sound like Henry James. But like most complaints of this kind, this one is not only merely partially correct but also a compliment of sorts. After all, Henry James was a pretty classy guy.

Still, in the case of Agnieszka Kuciak, you have to wonder. She uses over twenty *noms de plume* here; are they really just versions of her? Kuciak complicates things by supplying only Internet usernames instead of the usual binomials. It is as though, by conjuring a world in which people are too hurried to express fully their joy or their sorrow on parting and hastily tap out "LOL" and "CUL8R" instead, Kuciak's poets are now obliged to give us the fully-dimensional world that the texters can't or won't capture in their abbreviations.

But who are Kuciak's poets? "Pisces" is a fitness nut otherwise known as "the swimming poet"; indeed, she prefers swimming to reading, which may explain why she lost a court case involving plagiarism (a victim of post-workout fatigue, surely she simply forgot to cite her sources or perhaps persuaded herself that the words she borrowed were her own). "Kamila L.B." is a nun with what some might call delusional tendencies, though I urge skeptics to remember that St. Teresa of Avila was thought delusional by her detractors. The aptly-named "Doctus" is an obsessional footnoter of his own metaphors and, mercifully, "a rare example of an erudite poet."

So their lives are different—are their poems? We may as well begin with Doctus, whose "Ballad of the Pearl" begins:

Now pure, in search of heaven's heights,
she shot off from her bathtub into flight.

And bravely, her ethereal spirit soared
as far as the psychiatric ward.

A distinct voice, indeed! And surely one as great as that of the Scottish poet William McGonagall, author of "The Tay Bridge Disaster" and other under-appreciated poems in the Anglophone tradition. In marked contrast, there is the housewife-poet Mrs. K, whose work consists largely of salty observations on unreliable men. There is the resentful Sylvia, who could have easily composed song lyrics in grunge-era Seattle ("The vomited walls of your life stink. / Your dad's drunk and God's drunk"). And what do you think of when you read these lines by the proudly insane Schizus Christus?

We get no holy email, the Lord God
doesn't call, even on the ward.

Like me, did you not say to yourself, "By heaven, Schizus Christus sounds like none other than the love child of Gerard Manley Hopkins and Samuel Beckett!" Of course you did, and that is exactly the point: none of these poets sounds like Henry James or Agnieszka Kuciak or anyone other than their unique selves.

That said, they do share certain topics. Italy comes up regularly here, but what chilly Northern European doesn't love what Goethe called "the land where the lemon trees bloom"? Depression is a regular subject, as might be expected in poems written by poets rather than motivational speakers or soccer coaches. The idea of resurrection shows up often as well; then again, who doesn't want to be reawakened, reinvented, given a new and vital life? It goes without saying that there are a number of poems that deal with romance, and you shouldn't be surprised if you find yourself shouting "Hot pants!" à la

James Brown on one page and dabbing at your eyes with a hanky on the next.

In sum, the poets of *Distant Lands* engage gumptiously with the one subject that is the province of all seekers, namely, that haphazard compound of whimsy, hope, despair, and flawed beauty we call human nature. The question, then, is not "Who are these poets?" but "Who are we?" These poets don't have the answer—no poet does—but you do, reader, and these poets, like poets everywhere, will help you find it.

—David Kirby

Translator's Introduction

Agnieszka Kuciak's *Distant Lands: An Anthology of Poets Who Don't Exist* is a tour de force. This faux anthology of twenty-one invented poets, with their poems and biographical notes, belongs in the company of world literature's distinguished fabulists—Jorge Luis Borges, Fernando Pessoa, Franz Kafka, and Italo Calvino—in blurring the boundary between the textual and actual worlds. It includes a certain "N. Miłosz," who like his late namesake, the Nobel Laureate Czesław Miłosz, is considered "the bishop of poetry," and the confessional poet "Sylvia," reminiscent of Plath. There's also the devotional housewife poet "Mrs. K" whose work can be heard on the conservative Catholic station Radio Maria; "Bionda," the scholarship holder to Italy, accused of committing a "great literary sin against the Holy Spirit," and "Pisces," an athlete-poet who only agrees to "perform her work in cities where she has access to a pool."

In contrast to the work of earlier Polish poets such as Miłosz, Wisława Szymborska, and Zbigniew Herbert, Kuciak's book feels removed from the tragedy of World War II and the trauma of the communist era. Now a member of the European Union, her Poland is marked by buying and selling, global Internet culture, and a Catholic hierarchy bent on preserving its influence. Her invented poets reveal deep divisions in Polish society—rather like the culture wars in America since *1980*—between those who espouse a worldly, secular identity and those who favor a purely Polish, Catholic one. But even two of the country's Romantic poets, Adam Mickiewicz and Cyprian Kamil Norwid, whose work helped sustain Poland when the country was partitioned for over a century, get a satirical makeover in this text. Kuciak updates a well-known Mickiewicz ballad by setting it in a chat room, and has Norwid inventing premises for a reality show.

An esteemed translator of Dante and Umberto Eco into Polish, Kuciak often uses Italy as a foil for Poland. The poet "Pilgrim," not unlike some of the worldly souls in the *Inferno*, calls for a Catholic "siesta," complete with a "lobster fast" and a "striptease for the soul." And the poet "D.A.," in a wink to Dante Alighieri, has created a series of "resurrection rhymes," which depict ordinary Polish citizens—a workaholic, a skeptic, a klutz, and even a layabout named Agnieszka K.—attempting to rise from the dead. In the satirical poems in *Distant Lands,* Kuciak seems to be indicting the dogmatic, nationalistic aspects of contemporary Polish Catholicism, even as in others, she evokes the mysticism and rituals associated with that faith.

The rhymes in the poems—some quiet, others flamboyant—suggest Kuciak's love of Polish cabaret, in which poets like Agnieszka Osiecka *(1936-1997)* penned "singing letters" and journalistic "reports in rhyme." When read alone, the poems in *Distant Lands* offer nuanced meditations on mysteries of existence—old age from the perspective of a child, the sudden onset of depression, questions about life after death. But when read with the poets' bio notes, the poems acquire ironic resonance. This play with perspective that allows Kuciak to be both wittily ironic and seemingly sincere reminds me of Umberto Eco's remark that in the postmodern age, we can no longer simply say, "I love you." We have to say, "As Barbara Cartland would say, 'I love you.'"

Bronisław Maj, poet and professor of Polish philology at Jagiellonian University in Krakow, has praised Kuciak's faux anthology as a "colorful yet precisely harmonized choir, fascinating in its richness and variety. And, paradoxically, in its unity: there isn't a single moment when we forget who's really speaking through the mouths (words, fates, emotions, thoughts) of these 'nonexistent' poets."

— Karen Kovacik

Foreword

The "distant lands" alluded to in the title are simply places where we don't go. Many poets can be found there—yes, all the charming psychotics, Italophiles and mystics, who never fully existed. The view of a well-known critic that "the sensationalism of their biographies makes up for the lyrical flatness of their poetry" derives from a certain misunderstanding. These poets don't have biographies per se, or even first and last names, just Internet usernames. Their poems and these usernames constitute this anthology, which the poets thought up themselves. As for those so-called "sensational biographies," they function as a sort of a virtual game. Today, when everyone wants to be someone else and somewhere else (in the Italy and Byzantium of the soul), this phenomenon makes sense. Yet it should be added that these poets, all made up and not really existing, bear a certain resemblance to each other. It's not unlikely that this anthology is simply the work of a gang of expert and cynical hackers, who hijacked the poems of some poor poet (guess who?).

—A.K.

Notes on the Authors

BIONDA

A scholarship holder, a student of beauty, who tends to flit here and there. God only knows what she did in Italy—maybe she went there to daydream? She has written a number of insignificant poems—in the words of one critic: "*Dolce far niente fa pensar niente.*" She goes to the library just to describe it, and she has made numerous trips to Rome largely to parody it. Her poem "In Rome" spurred protests from a certain Catholic radio station, which called it a "great literary sin against the Holy Spirit."

D.A.

Any resemblance of protagonists in the resurrection rhymes to people who still exist is not at all accidental. The "resurrection rhyme" as a literary genre possesses an eternal copyright.

DOCTUS

A rare example of an erudite poet: for each metaphor, he includes a yard of footnotes, for each poem a table in the appendix. He received a grant for his book from the Committee for Scholarly Research.

EROS XL

He seems to have had some mystical sexual experience, which scholars commenting on his work have compared to the conversion of St. Paul, after which he "gave himself over to beauty"—making love to women and writing poetry. Beyond that, nothing else is known about this poet.

KAMILA L.B.

Sister of the Norwidian order, who martyred herself on an account of the life and work of Romantic poet Cyprian Kamil Norwid. When the poet left for America and seemingly disappeared without a trace, she fell into an uncanny state, imagining herself to be his jilted fiancée, a certain Miss Kamila, who actually resembled Norwid, in his "forsaking of his very self." Her poems testify to the unstinting labor of academics and the low esteem in which that work is held.

LOLA

She takes seriously the notion of "the poet as perpetual child," a phrase she heard a lot as a girl whenever she went though growth spurts. Her rhymes, ponytails, short skirts worn well into her eighties, habit of rollerskating to poetry readings, and longterm relationship with a known pedophile all speak to the unanticipated consequences of that mantra. Laureate of the Order of the Diaper...

LYRIC POET

He comes off old-fashioned, exquisitely preserved in rhymes and meter, swathed in tasteful Italian landscapes and the idea of the baroque. His specialty is the literary postcard, the landscape conveying the soul in ecstasy. The press, however, recently revealed that this charming older gentleman lyrically molested underage girls, who were found afterwards to have been injured in the least lyrical parts of their bodies.

MRS. K (PANI KRYSTYNA)

is a homegrown poet who blooms in the kitchen. A caretaker of her family's feelings and the poor's, she's an exemplary wife and mother and a dedicated member of the Circle of Flying Housewives. Her poems have been broadcast on a certain Catholic station as part of the cycle "The Mysteries, Sorrowful and Joyful."

NEIGHBOR

Known as "the bard of our concrete homeland." Laureate of the Order of Fridays.

NOBODY

is a poet who believes she doesn't exist, has never existed, and will not exist in the future, a fact that has driven countless literary critics to distraction. They hold the view that this author, who's essentially good for nothing and writes poems that no one reads, could, out of politeness at least, have the grace to exist a little. Consequently, she's been mocked in the newspaper for her diet (oranges with pepper), her terrible French ("fox paws" for *faux pas*), and her "meteorologically conditioned Buddhism" (when the sun's shining, she reverts to Catholicism). Her nonexistence grows increasingly extreme...

N. MIŁOSZ

A poet of amiable faith, known as "the bishop of poetry." He has lyrically consecrated countless lakes and landscapes, and he believes in the holy baptism of ink, the sacrament of poetry readings, the poem as penance, and the grace that comes from literary prizes. He writes, however, only about God.

PILGRIM

Known also as "the poet of San Piero," he lived like a mendicant in "the Italy of his soul," where he supposedly experienced a mystical shock—or so say the skeptics—after eating an ordinary slice of good pizza. He typically begged for alms by the Basilica of San Piero, holding a sign that said: "I write poems and praise God in them." He possessed the grace of being able to heal with his shadow, and some believe he was a saint.

PISCES

Known as the "swimming" poet, she's inspired by the whole philosophy of fitness. She refers to metaphor as "the muscle of meaning" and poetry itself as "linguistic calisthenics." A certain well-known critic has noted, "She's among those poets who no longer read, who spend whole days swimming and only agree to perform their work in cities where they have access to a pool." Her poetry is known for its pithiness, muscularity, and courage; however, some of that courage has deserted her now that she lost a court case for plagiarizing lines and metaphors. (Somehow underwater she must have read something?)

P.P.

That is, "poet of the abyss" or "screwed up psyche" or theoretician of "creative suicide." His poems have been banned by the psychological censor of this "distant land," where "he doesn't exist." His deeply suicidal poem "And death, not you, will gaze through your eyes" is the only exemplar of his dark legacy to survive. In his words: "I was not dissuaded from reading, I didn't pay fines for metaphors, I refused to go to therapy every Sunday, and I did not submit to mandatory psychoanalysis. Despite constant surveillance, I never stopped making poems." This he wrote, seeking poetic asylum in our anthology.

REVEREND

A witty cleric, connoisseur of the Lord's Blood, even in nonliturgical settings; a traveler who "journeys to heaven only by way of Toulouse, London, Palermo and Florence." Equally capable as a priest and a poet. One mystery remains, however: why this urbane man of the world, elegant in dress and conversation, a distinguished authority on art, would condemn his heroine, clearly in some southern clime, to wear thick and ugly tights? This lapse in the area of feminine *dessous* no doubt attests to his commitment to celibacy.

SCZHIZUS CHRISTUS

A schizophrenic poet, whether a recovered schizophrenic or one who persists in the delusion that he is, no one knows. Popular with the media, this "professional lunatic" has developed a reputation in psychiatric circles as "a walking advertisement for psychotropic drugs." His poems, almost exclusively religious, have become a real cross for the Church to bear.

SOMEONE ELSE

A poet of the people who creates portraits of others, known for his pseudotranslations and literary mystifications. He had to invent 20 literary characters to express "his own" views. The less charitable believe that beneath his mantle of objectivity and empathy lurks a deep narcissism, and in reality, he writes only about himself.

STUDENT

Known in Krakow as the Polish department's poet, she believes in the concept of "poetry as revenge against the reader." Instead of studying for her exams, she tends to write satires of her examiners. A person who remains unreliable...

SUNNY

and is married to a brunette. (The editors regret that the rest of the contributor's note for this poet was wiped out by the I Love You virus.)

SYLVIA

A poet of resentments, rather like Dostoevsky's "evil and sentimental" protagonists, but shallow as a pond of tears. At base the picture of psychological health and physical good fortune, she has, for financial reasons, invented a difficult childhood, an alcoholic father, an addict mother, and alleged emotional disorders (aided and abetted in all this by her family, who share the copyright). Cynically, she believes that poetry is the "last mendicant order," and "readers listen to poets only out of pity."

TIRESIAS

A poet of women's portraits and inwardly, a woman himself. He believes in "poetry as an operation of change," and that includes sex, his variety of "lyrical transsexualism."

I.
The Rain Knocks Long on Everything

Fermata

The Po glides by before me—with the paradox
and parasol that made me pause here
in the lashing rain. There on the other side
lies a hill, a convent cloistered by trees,
and I vanish between an unknown
Italian and my left angel
in anticipation.
                    Before I lose my way
I open my palm to the moment's cool spray.

—*Nobody*

* * *

The rain knocks long on everything,
asking, "You there?" and I say, "No,
not at all." The rain is a master of Zen.
Maybe let loose from the heavens
like one sheer hand clapping?
Have a seat and listen
to this lesson on the house:
Whoever doesn't tend his garden
will be overrun by a wild, wild god.
In vain, repeat after him
the tiny, quiet "Yes"
that will destroy you.

(Drop by stubborn drop, like on that big night,
when the street vendor tried to sell us roses
but we didn't want any roses,
we wanted life itself.)

—*Nobody*

Canticle of the Lake

In this, water resembles grace:
it lightens our daily load.
—Mrs. K

It's not life, but how you swim through it:
to perform your Heraclitean rituals with a splash,
those rites as sundry as fish.

You can swim while crying as if on the cross
of the lake's long mirrors, in the silver laughter
of waves, your tears salting the sea.
You can swim like an embryo—in the dark, eyes closed,
in the white coastal fog, the watery gold of dusk,
attended by gulls, the yellow leaves of September,
like a fervent burst of rain, in prayer
folding your hands and bowing down,
rubbing against your sister-fish.
It's like making love and being born,
it's like what *is* had already passed away.

Learning to swim, you learn how to die.
When we die, heaven will lift our load from us,
and we, instead of time, will glide by.

Plato was wrong: the soul does not have wings.
It has gills and silver scales.

—*Pisces*

* * *

Verrà la morte e avrà i tuoi occhi.

[Death will come, and it will have your eyes.]

—Cesare Pavese

And death, not you, will gaze through your eyes.
What's faith but baptism in the black depths
of those pupils? Death will peer through them.
The eyelids will lower their merciful curtains
on our lives. Night will come on.
And death, not you, will gaze through your eyes.
Because you will be gone.

—*P.P.*

A Former Buddhist Addresses the World

Observe the bee, how he powders his tiny head,
making little calluses on the callas.
But this isn't Zen, today he's just slacking,
a disciple of summer. I used to want
to be rooted in God's navel
like a Siamese twin. Now I prefer him a bit further,
at his Word's length. And the bee, as bees do,
powders his plush head with a lurch,
as if about to buzz off to church.

—*Someone Else*

Faith

> In the cornfield, the light gleams so unreal
> as if each ear revealed a vista of gold.
> —Lyric Poet

This landscape: a road between hills,
stone-pines hovering over it like oracles,
the air heavy as if brushed with gold
from the wings of a Byzantine altarpiece.
In silence, the cicadas intone some eternal verse.
From the depths of a well hollowed out
of heaven, the long *addio* of a bell is wrung.

One may not enter there, except to glance
over the tall shoulders of mirrors and dreams
left ajar, yet everything can be found there:
fragrances and incantations and unicorns
of language. There what dwells
seems so profuse, it doesn't have to be.

—*N. Miłosz*

The Lyric Poet Considers the Lake

Clean as the drowsy line of fate
is the lake's shoreline, the line of reeds and trees.
And just like in words where you discern the truth,
in water you can glimpse heaven's depths, cushioned
in clouds. It seems we can plummet there without fear,
and the fisherman with his pliant line and pole
is reeling in something from the absolute,
but he's on vacation: it doesn't interest him.

He'd prefer two kinds of carp: Crucian and Common.

—*N. Miłosz*

Stones and Us

In the Middle Ages it was known, the hard depths
of our souls persist beyond our mortal selves.

Like stones in the garden,
they exist, and that's it.

The sun warms them, they cool at night.
They don't desire life or the fullness of being.

When I hold my breath, when I'm not in love,
I'm like them. And that's how I'll be
in death's husk.

Warmed by the sun, cooler at night.
Delivered from daily striving. For eons.

Consider this: what sort of savior
would come to redeem stones, and from what?

Well, believe that if you want, but to be constant
like them is what we should seek, to be ready.

Pebbles look on us with calm eyes,
through closed lids. Abiding.

—*Pisces*

II.
The Master of Detachment

From Childhood

It was like a scarecrow for storms,
that black umbrella. Just seeing it I'd burst
into rain. Its wire-lined, watertight abyss
swallowed up many a houseguest.

—Lola

Playing Hooky on a Holy Day

That the devil lurks in wait for the best—
even the Lord God himself—every child knows.
So escaping from him to the lake
was less a matter of logic than fear.
Even swimming, we folded our hands
in prayer and bowed deep. And that bitter taste:
was it the burn of heaven on our palates?
the clouds in judgment? the watery mirror
we swallowed? That fizzing in the water—
like powdered lemonade dissolving—
was the sound of our childish souls. Spoiled kids!
We deserved to be punished:
an apocalypse, a burning bush.

—N. Miłosz

Little Girl Wants to Be a Big Granny

To be that old, as if scrawled
in cuneiform, practically immortal.
Evenings, to knit a world
where warmth abides.

To be kissed now only like an icon,
suited for fervent bursts of prayer.
Like an elegy wrapped in rawhide
passed down from someone, who is me.

And even with closed eyes to see
a world of beauty, not black as pupils,
but brisk as Brighton's weather, Pontormo's paintings,
the color of parting, steeped in one's whole life.

A life spun out like a huge net
for golden fish.

—*Someone Else*

A Fable About Pain

Pain's like the sea—comes on in salty waves,
its touch like clammy fish, your vista blank.
You slip from it onto sunny sand,
a bearded grandpa spinning out a yarn.

—Mrs. K

* * *

That Daddy's larger than this life
I've always known. He taught me to vault
across fields of darkness like the knight
in chess, so now I leapfrog over his faults.

When he scared us with his Polish tequila,
when he cut off the priest's current,
he farmed me out to an encyclopedia
of relatives unrelated to him.

That Daddy's larger than this life
I've always known. If not for him, who then
would have thrown me in my first lake
so I'd swim far lower than his depths?

—*Lola*

Poet

He inhales the whole, gritty world.
Rough drafts he smokes with a filter
and into the air releases sentences
rounded and hazy as rings of smoke. Truth,
coiling into view, appears in a cloud.
A shower of ash falls on the Pompeii
of his ashtray.
                                        And from his tight-lipped home
he dispatches a word like a child for bread,
which though responsible and bent on its mission,
will wander through the streets of many pages, forget
what it came for, buy a sweet nothing
and lick it down to the very stick.

—*Someone Else*

Wife
(a theological epigram)

She waits for him like the congregation
waits for Christ. And like temptation.

Alas, the aforementioned husband
is late again, just becauseband.*

—Mrs. K

* In Polish, this final word is a hybrid of "ponieważ" (because) and "mąż" (husband), with the implication that it's the husband's prerogative to show up late or not at all.

Parable

She who didn't want to sew her wedding gown
from a parachute will maybe someday drop down
on the far side of heaven in its pretty folds.

And she who kept a key to the elevator door
for a building that no longer exists
will one day ascend to the terminal floor.

She who could tame at will
the cloud over this seething pot of potatoes—
it's as if she sat here with us still.

—*Mrs. K*

On Losing My Third Pair of Sunglasses

A nineteenth-century ball. A forebear's sweaty palm,
concealed beneath a *chapeau claque,*
tucks not a shirt but a fashion-plate's train
against his fly. The flightiness in Zosia's line
dates back to this opera-hatted rake.

And tales abound about grandmas who baked
gold watches in the batter of their cakes,
so as to foretell the hour of their deaths
(and thus remember what they might forget).

This year, as it happens, I've been bent
on losing shades of my shadow,
a master of detachment.

—*Mrs. K*

* * *

To drop oranges into his grave
out of sheer flightiness—what a *fox paw!*
And in the mind of this Poznań woman
a battle rages: whether to jump after
that bagful of orange suns
(dearer since bought on the cheap,
sweeter when eaten with pepper),
to descend like Orpheus, Aeneas, Dante
to the newly departed? Then to emerge
among the startled mourners with the oranges,
instead of him?
                                        Or to remain graveside
and add to their grief her little pang.

—*Nobody*

III.
In the House of the Psyche

Ballad of the Pearl

Now pure, in search of heaven's heights,
she shot off from her bathtub into flight.

And bravely, her ethereal spirit soared
as far as the psychiatric ward.

Her alien heart felt sick at the world;
beside her tub, a grim taboret swirled.

No one knew from which silver county
prefects in scrubs pulled her into her body.

Why with a paperknife, and why at night,
did she dissect God, by lamplight?

Why burn this lamp in the body's crypt
that she floated above, seven flights up?

In the mollusk's shell, in the sea's black hoard,
a pearl was hidden, which a monster devoured.

There's only knowledge, hope, belief.
Dreams lit by stars and heaven's unease.

The cosmos a snake that strangles us in sleep.
Laugh, and he looms near with pills and cup.

The world's a dark house where we find a berth,
for years the soul is fettered to the earth.

No one knows the source of spells like these,
and those who don't will never be redeemed.

—*Doctus*

Depression

Many are dead to the world in the holy convent of Depression.
Insomnia is its rule, as is the silence of mortification,
relentless as the razor's black stigmata
or total fasting from the hormone of happiness.
They wish to rise to heaven—though not too fast—
on a hollow cloud of gas.

To be so dull, to suffer without Suffering.
To not have much to say over soup,
and only over dessert, to admit in therapy:

"At night when I can't sleep, I pray my bitter rosary.
And sense that someone's lying next to me
but there's less and less of him
in the pit of bedsheets.
I'll show him to Your Grace soon.
I know he's an angel.
The angel's the sign."

—*Sylvia*

A Little Ballad for AA

Home—known to peddlers door to door
but not to you. You go there only after hours

and bump into your dad at the threshold
of some abyss. He's babbling about God.

The vomited walls of your life stink.
Your dad's drunk and God's drunk.

They sway at the precipice between bed
and aquarium, the table raving, you half-mad.

The guest wipes his boots on your heart—out
of respect for the lady of the house.

Home—known to peddlers door to door.
In you, they hollow out long corridors.

—*Sylvia*

Church

Odd, how our cannibalism reveals itself:
like children or the sick, we partake
of this tidbit of Mystery. What we eat
has the papery taste of blank verse
and lurks in our mouths like sanctified snow.

And on Sundays, how odd our cowardice
when we don't confess our loneliness
or our neighbor's sin. And we breathe in
the Holy Spirit's fragrance—love and incense—
which brightens our cross-eyed hearts.

Besides these, no other miracles occur.
We get no holy email, the Lord God
doesn't call, even on the ward.
Still waiting for a transplant of our souls,
they see in our ecstatic visions
only the psychotropic communion host.

—*Schizus Christus*

* * *

I like to imagine this pepper mill
I picked up cheap is part of a happy story.

Someone broke it in, fed it the black grains
of that time, and sprinkled it over bread.

This little helicopter hovered each morning in the kitchen,
snorting pepper over a breakfast filled with laughter.

Yes, I like to imagine this story.
And to forget it's not my own.

—*Sylvia*

* * *

Whoever doesn't seek possessions or a loving touch
will reach the depths of the soul.
The world says:
There lie grains of meaning. Grains
from which wormwood grows and the abyss.

In fact, only the surface can save us.
No one drowning touches bottom.

There's no salvation without this.
Sunstone. The bloody truth of wine.

God's a cat, purring absolution
out of his solitude. The skin of the world
is his whole heart, or so medievals thought.
And the hand? Why it's ruffling
the fur of his heart.

—*Schizus Christus*

In the House of the Psyche

I have this delusion I'm alive and walking through the world
when in fact I'm lying in the house of the psyche.
It's people that appear to me here,
not angels. They speak in human words:
"Good morning, sir, what's up with you today?"
"Thanks for asking," I say. "The voices are up."
I still see shapes and colors, not in heavenly auras
but in ordinary daylight or dusk; all shades
of saintliness between God and Satan,
but not them. I touch one face so gently
as if Cain could not have killed Abel.
I'm happy without his manic ecstasy.
My hallucinations are so banal (grassy smell and chirp of swallows)
that the doctor listens to me, bored.
But suddenly he opens his maw
to tell me these "symmmptoms"
will soon disappear and I'll have nothing to complain about.
He assures me: "You'll have nothing."

—*Schizus Christus*

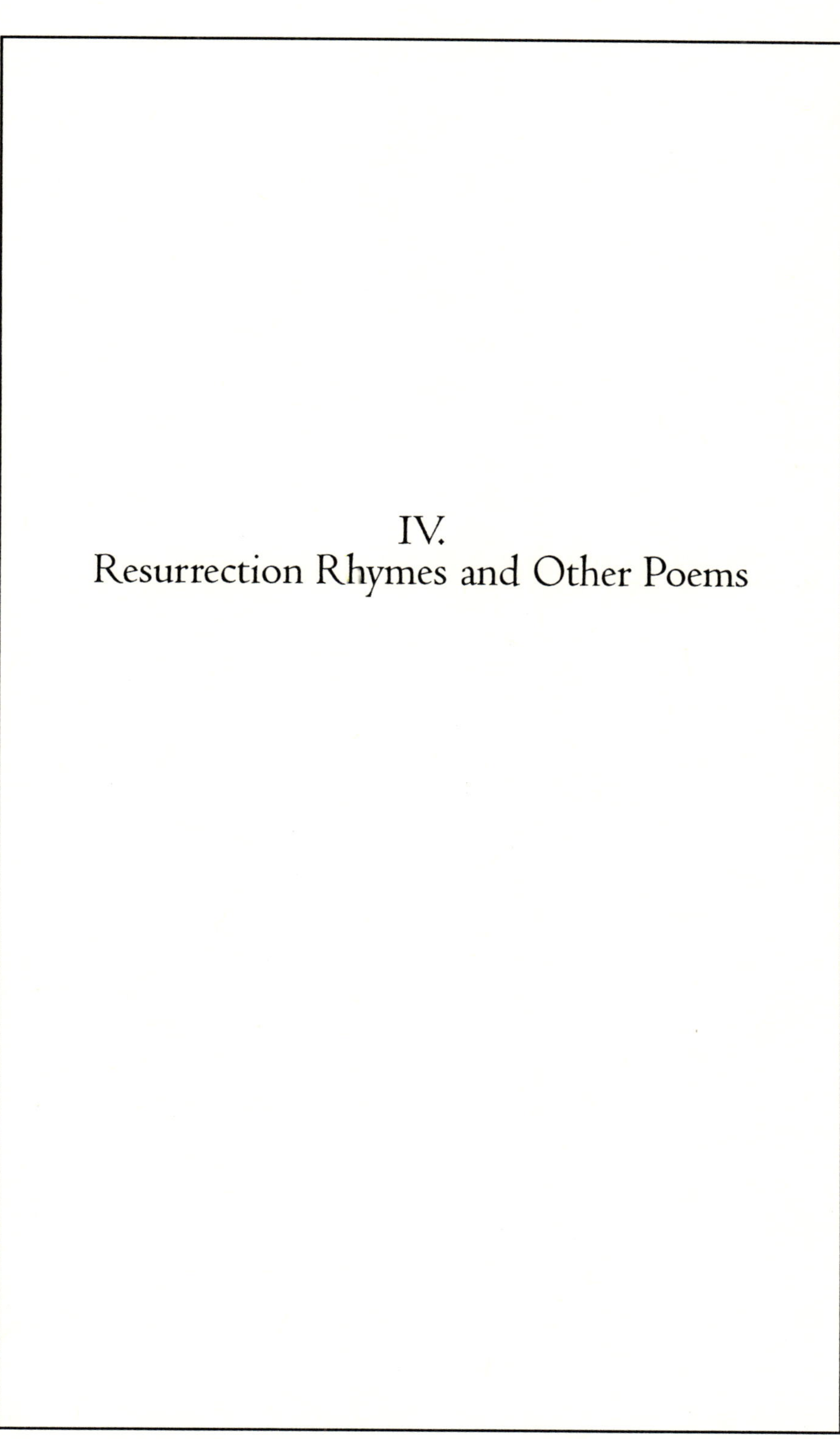

IV.
Resurrection Rhymes and Other Poems

Prologue

This Danticus* stood out among his kin:
one night he looked too long into his wine,
and then flew up to heaven, alive,
and there he witnessed unimaginable sights.

Chez God seemed fine, and so he sat a spell,
five centuries at least, to hear him tell,
and there had countless parleys with the Man,
though by and by he fell down to Poznań,**
where in a flash they locked him in the 'bin
because he kept expelling flaming wind.

After long chats about God, he heard them say:
"Trust us, this shot will help God go away."
How common, blah, blah, blah among psychotics,
to which Danticus murmured, "Oh you pr__ks."
And then he made a list, manic and hectic,
of those he saw in heaven resurrected.

—*D.A.*

* Johann Danticus, also known as Jan Dantyszek, was born in Gdansk in *1485* and died in Warmia in *1548*. For over thirty years a royal diplomat, he was also a bishop and poet, who wrote primarily in Latin. His most famous work was *Epitaph for Myself [Nagrobek sobie samemu]*.

** Poznań is a city in northwestern Poland where Kuciak lives.

I. Apocatastatic Rhyme on the Praiseworthy and Amazingly Well-Organized Resurrection of the Honorable and Resilient Miss Lydia N.

One eternal day, on an Advent morn,
an angel called: "Lydia, come to the Lord."
She glanced at her notes: "Eternal life?
It's already on my to-do list, chief."
Still, she demanded right off the bat
he produce the Boss's edict with six stamps.
He did. From the parish, all as it should be.
She said, "I knew this would happen to me.
In the grave, I took vitamins for the dead,
so my nose would look less red
for this occasion. I stand by my regimen,
that I rested—and decayed—according to plan.
So, aye, aye, Boss," she happily said,
then deftly, efficiently rose from the dead.

—D.A.

2. Apocatastatic Rhyme on Miss Agnieszka K., Unrepentant Sleepyhead, and Her Shameful Refusal to Rise from the Dead

'Twas very early one eternal morn,
a handsome angel blew upon his horn,
and whispered "Rise, Agnieszka" in her ear.
But that poor soul just drew her pillow near.
"God wants you close," he added, this time shrill.
She burrowed in her shroud as in a quilt,
then spoke as if emerging from a coma:
"My eyelids, sir, are suffering some trauma.
That God is waiting, sure, I can believe.
But let me rest a little longer, please.
No matter where, it's nice to snuggle in.
Eternal life's like one gigantic yawn."
The angel cried, and all the saints did, too:
Agnieszka in her grave refused to move.
She snoozed as if some soul had slipped her ether
until she felt the fires of hell beneath her.

What's to be done when called to paradise,
souls like Agnieszka K. just cannot rise?

—*D.A.*

3. Resurrection Rhyme on the Praiseworthy, if Uncertain Resurrection of the Erudite Miss Beata, a Very Skeptical Spirit

Humming hosannas, swathed in radiant robes,
God's angel flew right in to her abode.
Beata settled snugly in her vault:
worms ate at her, but so did utter doubt.
The angel said, "Dear, rise now from the dead,
for you are blessed and deeply loved by God."
Said she: "Rise just like that? You kidding, angel?
You'll have to bring me three encyclicals,
some holy books, and perpetual serials.
Before I rise, I'll need reading materials!
I won't forego my eternal ruminations—
in the grave at least, leave me time for contemplation."

Was she resurrected? The question has merit.
But even while dead, she surely read up on it.

—D.A.

4. Resurrection Rhyme on Ella's Praiseworthy, if Rather Insubordinate Rising (or Flight) from the Dead

An angelic type dropped by one day
to seek out Ella, long in her grave.
But lo and behold that charming lady
was not lying still, but flying and waving!
So the angel engaged her in a stern chat:
"Whose soul rose up illegally like that?
Whose spirit darts like a bee at dusk,
unsanctioned by me or any of us?"
Then loudly, the angel went on:
"To rise up by yourself: is that kosher?"
"Sorry," she replied, "some force came over
me, transcendental and arcane,
like no other I know and can't explain,
though indeed it came on quick and easy,
some inflamed mind's doing, a would-be
miracle, even if not sought by me."

She said her piece, then flew away,
like a good fairy or gold fly, some say,
or maybe a winged elf. I don't know,
just that Ella's raised up, and in church,
her spirit's flitting to and fro.

—D.A.

5. Apocatastatic Rhyme on the Praiseworthy Resurrection of the Rash, if Ardent Miss Zosia D.

Lying in her grave, dead but content,
she was hailed by an angel, heaven sent:
"Imagine, Zosia, my boss, the Lord
is calling you." She answered: "I'm on board."
But either the coffin had too sharp corners
or she leapt to the task with too much fervor,
or a nail stuck out like the tine of a fork, see,
'cause she tripped on the threshold to eternity.
And thus she played a different role:
instead of rising from the dead, she fell.

—D.A.

6. Resurrection Rhyme on the Praiseworthy Rising from the Dead by the Honorable Jerzy B.

"Rise up, Jerzy," said an angel near his tomb,
though that youthful rose had lost his bloom.
"This way to paradise." But Jerzy squawked:
"Maybe in a week? Today I'm overbooked.
I still have odds and ends to get done:
a record of my non-life to jot down.
So many tasks are weighing on my head,
while I comb through my archives of the dead."
The angel got worried and flew to his superior.
They waited two weeks, three, and even more.
A month, then six, but Jerzy still delayed:
"Lord, some other time, just not today."
How to handle him? John Paul II offered this:
"His corpsely record has been meritorious.
Even the worms hold him in high regard
for how he's decomposed in the graveyard
along with his papers, providing matter
for stimulating and learned patter.
Give him another chance." They took his advice,
and Jerzy B. has toiled that day to this.

Our aunts and uncles put it best:
"First comes work, and then comes rest."

—D.A.

7. Resurrection Rhyme on the Less Than Exemplary Rising from the Dead by the Witty Doctor Marek D.

One eternal day, quite warm and lyrical,
an angel came calling, a true miracle
of grooming and tact. "Dear sir," he said,
"would it please you now to rise from the dead?"
But Marek replied: "My nerves aren't great.
Can't I please just have a little break?"
Thanks to eternal life's new stress,
he desperately craved the cigarette
his trusty kin had placed in his pocket,
along with a flask and a phrase in a locket.
So he smoked, Lord, he smoked, with all his soul
like those who aren't in the grave at all.
And then, dear reader, he guzzled the liquor
as if falling off the wagon forever.
But at the phrase "Smoke, drink, and be merry"
poor Marek looked lost, since there was nary
a soul to make merry with. So feeling downcast,
he turned back to the grave instead of the sack.
Because the day was so lyrical and bright,
no coffee was offered, the angel too polite.

—D.A.

8. Resurrection Rhyme on the Right Honorable Radoslav's Heroic Lingering in the Grave

The Lord's angel dropped by so at least once
Radoslav might treat him to a decent lunch
with a meat course. He said, "Rise up, Radoslav."
And Radek blinked, then glanced above
and around to see if in the vicinity
lurked some leftists maybe,
and after a moment, ascertained there were.
If he were the cursing sort, "hell" is what he'd swear
because that night was the debut, dammit,
of a certain—cruel joke indeed—structuralist.

So he dashed off a note, emphatic in its prose,
"In reckoning my strengths and many flaws,
I beg you, gracious Lord, to bestow
this resurrection on some better fellow."
And feeling a weight upon his heart,
he again moved to depart
underground to his grave, where, still dead,
he practically lost his head,
waiting for a response from God.

His cheeks are pale, it's said,
and a terrible lassitude
came over him, so he hid
in a haystack, dismayed
as if the world had ended dot, dot, dot...
But I know better: he's not too blue
since in heaven he can get *Ars Longa Review.*

—D.A.

A Lighthearted Complaint to Our Creator, Regarding the Devilish Inventions of Our Times

At night, when I turn on my TV set,
who knows what ungodly scenes I'll get.
Creative, Lord, the devils you gave us
like the demon who dreamed up these ads to assail us!
There's the woman with broom who steals out of sight,
though it's no witches' sabbath, just Saturday night.
This same woman claims: "My house is immaculate!
There's a pit by my bed and I sweep the dust into it."

Oh God Almighty, what a terrible habit:
to praise the abyss as a timesaving benefit!

—*Mrs. K*

For Hannah

Blessed Hannah of the apartment house feeds stray cats
and while doing her mopping, meditates.
She scrubs the hall like her own soul,
and I have to admit, that to one and all,
even the one who puked on the stairs,
she says "Good Day" like her morning prayers.

—*Neighbor*

Norwid*

> who, according to reliable accounts of his life and work, bathed maybe twice in his life, and never before cameras, now comments from beyond the grave on our obsession with "reality" everything

Recipe for a popular show? Set up a camera in the toilet.
Or before a crowd of viewers, shoot
a sex scene—as in Petrarch's dream.

Who cares if literary types look down their nose at it?
While shooting the nose, be on the lookout for snot,
then come in close with the zoom!

—*Kamila L.B.*

* Cyprian Kamil Norwid (*1821-1883*), one of Poland's Romantic poets

Lady Kills Gent
(an electronic ballad)

A crime without precedent:
some lady kills her gent.
She cuts off odds and ends,
and plays with them in bed.
An anchor on TV
sparked these gruesome fantasies.

And later that whole night,
she guts the body right,
with a spritz of salt and pepper,
then grinds the flesh like paper.
She feeds her kids the meat,
then searches on the net
to hatch her grisly plans
to market his organs.

Alas, she soon got caught,
she spent too long in chat.
Her husband's bro logged on
to that same chat anon.

And then the FBI
pursued her all July.
At last, they pulled her in
while she was drinking gin.

Like a patch of lilies fair
beckons the electric chair.
Fairer still the strapped-in body
for a scientific study.

—*Kamila L.B.*

V.
To San Piero

To San Piero

The sea is light as wine.
The marble, catlike, murmurs in the sun.
In the basilica, bowls of light
float between the columns.
The well-read beggar doesn't notice
God has tossed into his cap
that day's gold coin.

My road leads to San Piero.
Here Nicodemus was destined
to slip from the belly of Eve.
His walls are a membrane of angels
and happiness. And one room over,
Shiva still dances his dance
of forest light. He will long
for this moment in moments of longing.

My road leads to San Piero.
Here Saint Peter's shadow will make me whole.
But when I say my name, I feel in my blood
the ancient Sanskrit flame of sadness.

—*Pilgrim*

In the House of Ugolino

Books abound in the palazzo Gherardesca.
On the famine tower, you'll see a bell and old clock,
and all along the interior, a library
with an underground entrance to the other side,
the eternal one, framed by a hairy demon's
illuminated legs. This labyrinth of books
is the only paradise.

From there, you return to the world
as if from the land of *non omnis tornar*
under the arcade of the Guelphs
where there should be a bistro "Ugolino's Place,"
because of all who cut their teeth there,
testing his teeth, claiming
he actually drank wine and ate shrimp.

Even the number of dead children
seems not so important after a little wine.
Later, near the Arno, a beggar sells us a minute
maybe two, of compassion—an unending siesta.
Our world becomes "Dante, Canto IV."

And Ugolino? He remains in the library
where he sucks brains dry.

—*Bionda*

Duomo

Not for the light, not for glimpsing from afar
His Radiance through faith's stained glass,
but for refuge does one seek out this eternal place.

Retreat from the penetrating sun to the coolness
of the crypt, to *chiaroscuro* and the columned dark.

A clock hangs there, a painted horse.
The poet holds the keys to three countries.*
Original sin billows from the confessional,
and Portinari's daughter, in her red dress,**
has round, full breasts.

This is where God goes for his siesta:
he wolfs down a crisp host with spinach
and sleeps so soundly he'd have an alibi
if charged with assailing Saint Paul at noon.

—*Pilgrim*

* This line refers to the painting *Dante and the Divine Comedy* by Domenico di Michelino, which hangs in the Duomo of Florence.

**Beatrice Portonari, the woman Dante loved

Et in Arcadia

A cypress path curves through this world.
Above it night birds wail, and there beneath
the orange sun, a tranquil scene unfurls,
to which one flees surveillance of the soul.
Beyond it one envisages the sea,
a Rome of troubled love or river swells
or pain, perhaps, though no one's sure.
Beyond the cypress path death dwells.

—Lyric Poet

Venerdi santo

On this day of agony and Venus—and joy and sorrow and theater:
the main hero dies.

He can't taste the blood and wine on his lips,
but feels the gaping wound and wood gone deaf.

There's a void in the liturgy, and Saint Peter's cast as a brunet
destined for love and betrayal.

"Just say the word," we repeat, "and I shall be healed."

How marvelous that such a word exists, marvelous
that rhetoric and sculpture have not yet been banished.
The faithful of this divided homeland
give off the odor of seafood in church, and beneath a Corinthian column,
the scent of the morning rose cut from marble.
They're on a first name basis with mystery.

And how marvelous that *trecento* angels, fainting under the weight
of their gold haloes, loom side by side with muscular porters
from a heaven scalpeled into slices.

It's not so easy to paint shadows, according
to the laws of perspective, especially ones that can heal.
Nor to believe in death, which is not really death.

—*Pilgrim*

* * *

Like a skull memento, the plane-tree dryad's
striptease is a prayer fit for this world.

A liturgy of sun, earth, sfumato.
The honeyed breath of amber meadows.

Blue hills, the hush of cypress groves;
high up, the forest's boon of leaves.

The hour of long shadows, golden light.
A liturgy of air and water, followed by

the liturgy of the word, like a stone
in the sea's entrails, burnished and honed.

—*Lyric Poet*

* * *

In you, the world scars over like a wound of the sea,
though it's to the sea you run to cry, to swim
till your arms ache, and beyond.

The body thrown into the sea—what it means
depends on what you can imagine.

The sea's as full of chasms as a house is full of drawers—
salt strewn from every shaker onto a platter of fish
bordered by the sky.

There, the entire religion consists of folded hands,
the entire art—*l'arte del tornar.*

There a jellyfish, like a mandarin of the sea,
bedazes with his majesty. And in the dark's deep maw,
a horrific barracuda gorges on glistening things.

On the shore, their eyes will darken
when you fail to return.

—*Schizus Christus*

* * *

Sure, I'll rent out to others all my dreams,
with magnolias and a garden seen through glass,
a quail's flight erasing the tableau
where many dwelled, but never you.

My dreams feel light and clear. A table waits
with plates of cuttle-fish, where they will eat,
where a man will enter a woman through a veil
of words woven by me.

—*Bionda*

"Where Can We Live But Days"

As if passing through the fire of ancient legends, words
sent from beyond the grave thaw in the flames:
"Where can we live but days?"
They're bolted fast forever.

We're silos destined to be steeples.
On our skin, time traces the bones
of our changes. We dream of Florence.
God touches us only with his shadow.

And days hover at the horizon, during twilight,
across the fragrant earth, in transit, our eyes open wide.
Days have borders but no bottom.

We have to let the dead recede
to hold them close.

—*Pilgrim*

Solo grazia

Our brilliant Lord is like an Italian
from Rome: he requires
a Catholic siesta.

Other religions are not allowed here.
Fevered seas roil beneath a sun of salt.

Artemis will not live in a bottle
of *extra vergine,* and no genie in wine.

Here faith and a lack of illusion commingle.
Liturgical vestments and a striptease for the soul.
Sister Jism and a lobster fast.
God's bordello. A sommelier of our Lord's blood.
And the brains of saints, that they may be touched.

What sin might this landscape not absolve?
When the sea glitters, there's no remedy.
There's only the grace of peering at the sun
through alabaster crests.

Or being beloved of bones, in beggar's rags,
toothlessly, like that old woman from Cefalù.

And no one knows why Leopardi came here
carrying the world on his hump like a black shadow
at the high noon of his life.

—*Pilgrim*

At Saint Peter's

I have a room at St. Peter's and eat ice cream—
the flavors out of this world.

I wake lightly when tiny sparrows drop by
in the morning with their tangle of wings.

After I down a few glasses of wine, paradise
draws near to this basilica

where Peter blessed the cubist oaks
lining the avenue of *sua santità,*
where happiness dwelled and storms blew in at dawn
each time the sea shivered.

At St. Peter's I have a peaceful room
and a beauty not of this world.

—*Pilgrim*

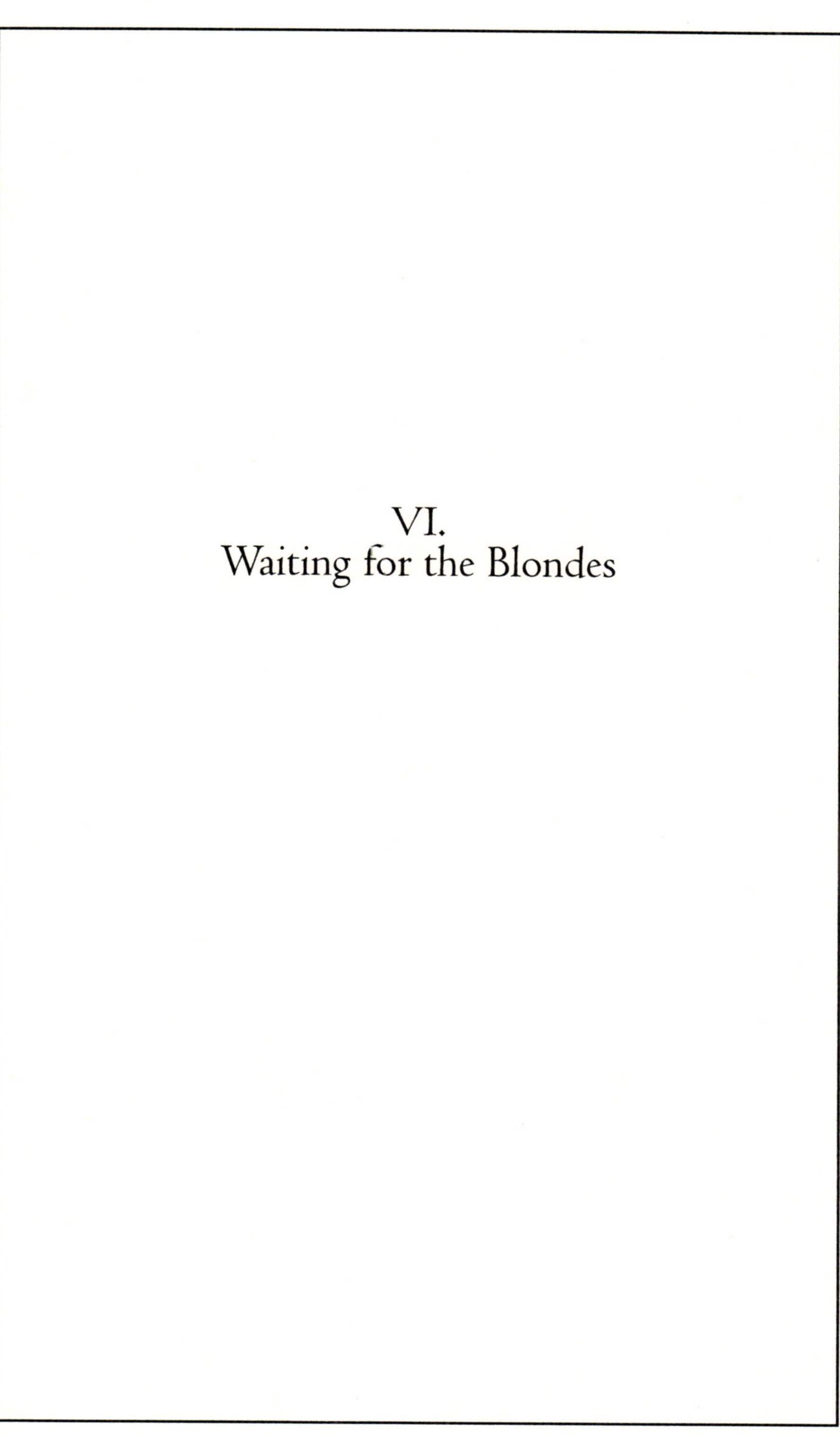

VI.
Waiting for the Blondes

By Bernini

This graceful Daphne bolts out of fear, baroque
and blossoming. To the gods, give thanks

that you survive. She's distant now, always eluding;
in marble, she transitions to a laurel evading

a god, as well as your body and gaze.
She flees ever deeper into heaven's haze

beyond sex. Let the angel in the sculpted air
capture this marble nymph in wild prayer.

—*Lyric Poet*

The Slavicist's Song

What brought her here in such a wild guise,
hungry among the books, galaxies
without touch, among his concerns,
his *idées*? Not passion, but pattern,
the stubbornness of rhyme, and apropos, her tits
protruding in a manner most un-Catholic.
She's formidable as a warden, rash as a corrida.
He takes refuge in laughter, that volume of Norwid, a
lovely, skintight bibliographic note
its only attire. He doesn't want her. Even she'd admit
she didn't want him to want her. Her soul so small,
on the shelf of Dostoevsky it wouldn't fit at all.
Let her run off to some other novel.
What brought her here in such a wild guise,
hungry among the books, galaxies
without touch, where the heart shivers
only from cold, where dreams freeze over?

—*Student*

Romance

She made a mistake. She wanted to be loved
for her soul's exquisite fragrance, and not Yves Saint Laurent.

The soul's fragrance was best stored in books,
in crypts of paper. But there was too much suffering in the soul
to push them past death's breathless limits.

She made a mistake. She wanted to be loved
for her words' décolletage, but she didn't have any.

So how was she supposed to meet him between the lines
that leaked from every text and every toilet
on a corridor lit by gas lamps?

If only she were well-endowed with bibliographic beauty,
which would eclipse that beauty "beyond words."

She made a mistake. He didn't fall in love.
He got lost in his reading, but not in her.

—*Student*

La moto

The ground rushes by so fast, the soul,
like a rocket, belches fire from below.

I hold on tight to you with my knees
so I don't plunge into the air.

—Bionda

* * *

Naked, she let me in a secret gate.
Through it I crossed
to another world.

The moon gleamed, and there she lay
like a silver spoon for sipping the moon.

Naked, she let me in a secret gate.
Through it I crossed
to another world.

The moon gleamed, and there she lay,
a dainty silver fork for eating the stars.

Naked, she let me in a secret gate.
I wanted to slip through it
to return home.

But there I saw the world, the moon, and her.
Like a silver knife for carving the moon.

She stood, covered the opening with her light dress,
and left me forever
I don't know in what world.

—*Eros XL*

Italian Lover

Blundering onto her blondness, he wants her
and for a while, this world, the erection
of mountains, towers and moons.
His specialty: serial sex.

He knows how to pick up happiness
on the street, how beauty must be unearthed
with caresses beneath closed eyes
and fists of absolutely not.

Between a man and a woman,
there's only skin and skill.
The cooling bed lends them
this alone, without reproach.

—*Bionda*

Cashier from the Kiosk Writes to the Newspaper

My fingernails hint at rose-colored romance
but unfortunately, they tally only tickets.
I cloak my voice in velvet
to say: *That'll be two fifty.*

Still I think positive: I beat out
Marie Claire, Mirabella, even Mademoiselle,
though they beckon more beautifully
(since they're not trapped behind plastic ponchos,
combs, lotions, cigarettes, tabloids, and the lotto!).

It's cramped here in my sad booth, no one sees me,
and the uneventful days drag on and on.

When will he come? Will he subscribe
to my desires? And will he wait
not just for change from a five
but for me?

—*Someone Else*

Portrait

She's alone again. It's like going out with someone
on a boat—doesn't matter who—
to sway with the indifferent stars.
Or tasting someone else's salt on her tongue
instead of her own bitterness, knowing now
the world is no instrument for love.
How listlessly the light lies down on her days,
without tenderness.

—*Tiresias*

Vocation

She kneels at the bed's precipice,
and no one knows how she'll jump
over Egypt, over her own heart,
that place aching after him.

She could be faithful to the one who didn't touch her.
She could be faithful to the one who is gone.

She could be like the others, drinking wine,
desiring this body or that, untransformed.

She's more and more faithful
the less faith she has.

—*Tiresias*

Waiting for the Blondes

Why these speedy scooters, this whiff of principles?
Why those hothouse muscles, those sunburned hearts?
Why do men's brains fill up with brilliantine
and dark glasses mask their dark eyes
as if to rush the onset of some tiny night?

What do Italian men do, as summer draws near?
Italian men wait for the blondes to appear.

Watch the blondes wring tears from the others,
all deserving as a legal dream—
the ones petite as demitasses, dark
as suspicion, lovely as their own rage.

What do Italian men do, as summer draws near?
Italian men wait for the blondes to appear.

They want the ones with Slavic sweetness,
full of charming grammatical errors,
the ones pale as daylight or the sky
when it's the color of tears.

What do Italian men do, as summer draws near?
Italian men wait for the blondes to appear.

Let the sun shine blond even on blondes.
And let them desire these foreign desires.
Let them aspirate the word "casa"
in the best Etruscan manner.

What do Italian men do, as summer draws near?
Italian men wait for the blondes to appear.

But blondes are like the sea breeze.
Blondes are hardly the solution!
After three kisses, all the blondes
lock down tight.

—*Sunny*

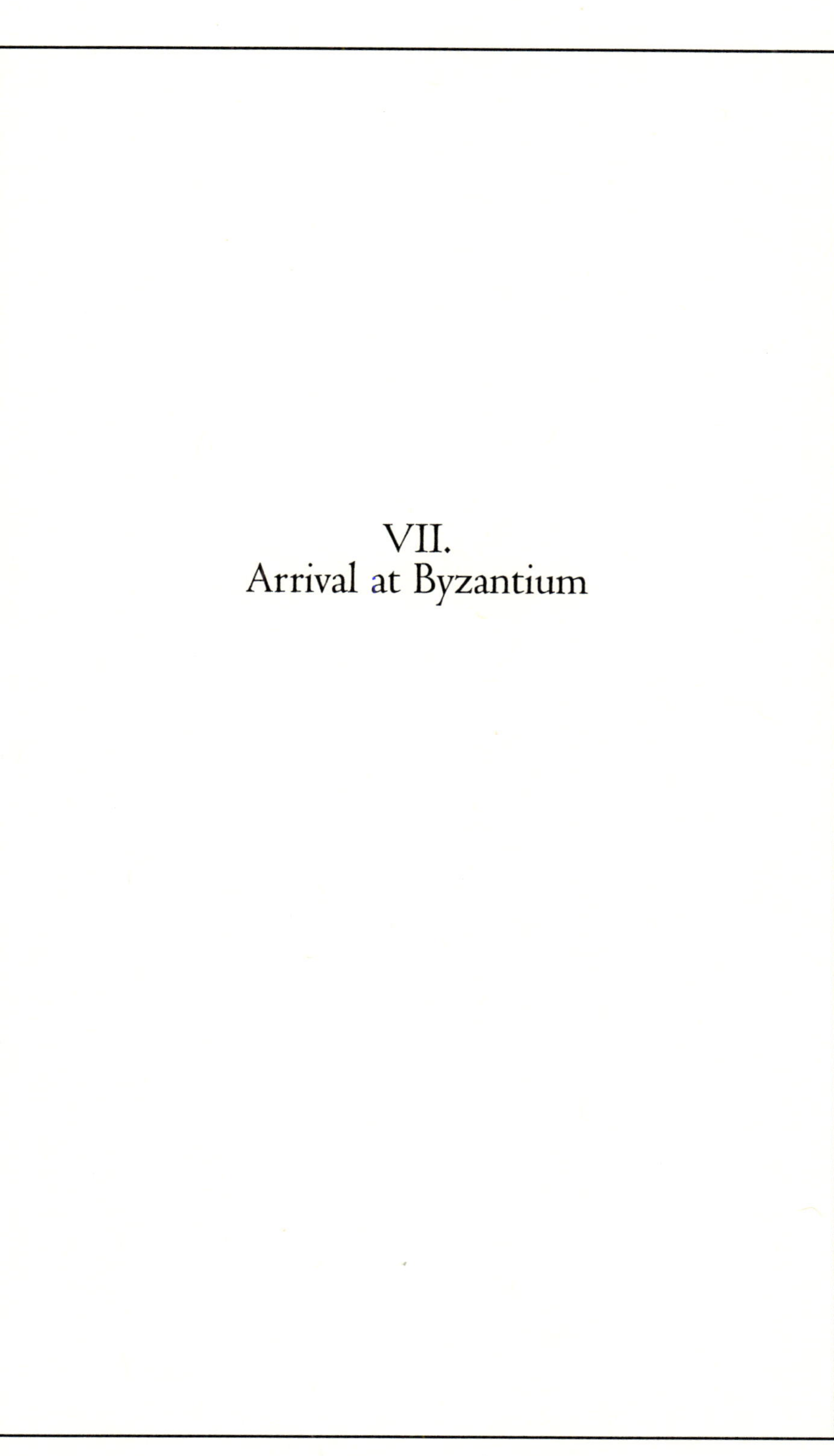

VII.
Arrival at Byzantium

In Rome

Here they drink in desire from every source.
Lovely eyes take in loveliness with each glance,
and in the holy city everything is holy.

Holy the Campari, holy the horses' marble tails
at the Capitol, holy the foot of Saint Peter,
which Christ once washed and centuries have blurred,
holy the voice of Callas in this dying church,
a former brothel. Holy, too, the mingling
of spirits at noon and bodies when darkness falls.

But where are those spirits? you ask. In the sun perhaps.
The demon of acedia appears only at the hour
when the cat's eye shrinks, when the world reins in shadow
like a monk his lust.

And the Holy Spirit breaks off
his anecdote and changes the plan.

—*Bionda*

Arrival at Byzantium

1987

This is no country for virgins. Market tents
adrift in desire, the vendors dreaming not
of eternity, but a night in the houris' den.
The icon of flesh trades now for banknotes,
she who inclined iconoclasts to sin.
Now cheap, despite the city's epic roots,
she gladly accepts tribute, and in her crystal vases,
smuggled from afar, beholds strange, distant places.

The tongue that slipped into a rosy ear
is the tongue of flame igniting the hands
of the icons' makers. In their hearts, after the fire
a deafness will take hold, like that
when Plato was banned (the emperor required
vows of obedience, not irony, from all minds).
The earth's a cupboard where God stores his hosts.
From a single word, a schism will explode.

In her vases, the icon sees everything
and herself, older than time. Wanton and content,
five sheets over the earth, she swings
her hips, and her chariot of fire ascends,
buoyed by grace. Against the sky's gold rings,
haloed Nike at her side, she'll never relent
in dogma wars with armies of arabesques.
Beside her an angel, a blue eunuch, basks.

—*Doctus*

From the Rectory

Sunday smells like cake and the Holy Ghost.
You have to air out the place after both.

No one can fill up on the host alone.
You have to eat something more solid.
He who hears confessions today
will soon be confessing her.

Mrs. K, the parish priest's dream,
winks coquettishly at the gold backdrop.
Pretty as a pot roast, she'll even knit
a halo, before being converted later.
For now, she remains resolved in faith
and scours not her sins
but crumbs off plates.

—*Someone Else*

Distant Lands

She followed after the man
selling distant lands.

Dressed for eternity, he bellowed:
"Hey, Mrs. K, pin your blonde hair in a halo.

Imagination's kingdom's not this bar,
a genie dribbling from some pint of beer.

Come and view your life beyond this one
as through a keyhole. Watch it fan

out like your heart's mosaic. Subsidize
your meager pension with paradise.

There an orange glistens and a lemon.
On the gold ground, the virgin bears a son,

and he gives birth to her on the other side,
the earth's tapestry a fiery brocade.

There, wings interlaced, float the seraphim,
and I'll take my leave of you at 'Amen.'

Go, Mrs. K. You'll see your husband soon:
undying, faithful. In a word, no goon.

I'll be there, too." She glimpsed her husband.
This time, he'd not gained weight again.

He smelled like incense and Dolce & Gabbana.
Shocked, her brows rose like hosannas.

He led her straight from the bar
to an unfamiliar autocar.

She passed rivers, hills, and golden sheafs,
the before and after of her whole life.

Till by Arethusa's tranquil stream,
her illusions snagged like her tights with seams.

The stream looked cloudy, like the dark brew
of her earthly past. And just as she had lived—askew—

she woke now from her life. She heard a voice,
not loud, rising from the sea: "O praise,"

it said. "Flee, nymph, into the dark if you're able,
or stay and lay your dreams on the mafiosos' table,

no matter if in error or on the ocean floor.
Imagination's kingdom is not here."

—*Reverend*

On Reading His Poems in a Church

The poet sits at the paschal table,
part monstrance, part monster.

Something is peering over his shoulder at the black letters,
as he gazes out at the baroque shadows.

How much can he say, really, sitting
with his back to the mystery, pouring not wine
but water into his glass, when the word gets dry?

He's among those who "love one another,"
who know less about beauty than whatever
springs to mind between the lines.

The audience doesn't detect this good spirit,
late for eternity, waiting
for more than an autograph.

—*Someone Else*

Translator's Acknowledgments

Thanks to Dennis Maloney of White Pine Press for taking on this project and to David Kirby for the lively preface that ricochets from Gerard Manley Hopkins to Seattle grunge to place Kuciak in an Anglophone context. Mira Kuś read the entire manuscript in Polish and English and helped me unlock the text's most stubborn syntactic riddles. Thanks, too, to Nin Andrews and Michael Martone for the votes of confidence. Nin also suggested how people who aren't Catholic might perceive the text, and Jim Powell finetuned the music. Bill Johnston's encouragement and logistical support, often over triple espressos, enabled me to push this project from manuscript to book. Ania Spyra kindly commented on some of the poems during our long bike rides up the Monon Trail. I'm also grateful to Olgierd Chmielewski and to Jerzy Illg of Znak Press in Krakow for permission to reprint Mr. Chmielewski's resonant cover art, which appeared on the Polish edition of Kuciak's book as well. Grants from the National Endowment for the Arts and the IUPUI Arts and Humanities Institute allowed me to travel to Poland and Italy to complete the translation and underwrote some of the publication costs as well. Katarzyna Boruń-Jagodzińska of Warsaw's Galeria Nigdy-Nigdy hosted a bilingual reading of selections from *Distant Lands:* thanks to Joachim Biernacki, Paweł Boruń-Jagodziński, Gosia Gabryś, Basia Kalestyńska, Bogdan Krawczyk, Mira Kuś, Joanna Multan-Świątkiewicz, Lana Santoni, Wayne Santoni, Krystyna Salitra, Steve Schubert and Ania Spyra for making that evening so lively and memorable. And to Agnieszka Kuciak, who once cited Rimbaud's phrase "*Je est un autre,*" I've so enjoyed spending time—and losing myself—in your gallery of many masks.

The Author

Agnieszka Kuciak is one of the most original younger poets currently working in Poland. Her debut volume *Retardacja* (Delay), published in 2001, established her as a poet devoted to elaborate forms and punning, to the blending of the classical and contemporary. *Distant Lands,* originally published in Poland in 2005, is her second collection. Kuciak is also an esteemed translator of Italian literature, who has brought Dante's *Divine Comedy,* the sonnets of Petrarch, and Umberto Eco's *The History of Beauty* into Polish. She won the Polish President's Prize for her scholarly monograph *The Romantics' Dante.*

The Translator

Karen Kovacik's translations have appeared widely in such journals as *American Poetry Review, Colorado Review, Crazyhorse, Southern Review* and *West Branch,* and in numerous anthologies. She has received a fellowship in literary translation from the National Endowment for the Arts and a Fulbright Research Grant to Poland. Her own poetry has been awarded the Charity Randall Citation from the International Poetry Forum and the Barbara Mandigo Kelly Peace Poetry Prize. *Metropolis Burning,* from the Cleveland State Poetry Center, is her most recent collection. She is currently editing an anthology of Polish women poets, *Calling Out to Yeti.* Kovacik directs the creative writing program at Indiana University Purdue University Indianapolis. In 2012-2013, she served as Indiana's Poet Laureate.